SPARKS OF LIFE

Chemical Elements that Make Life Possible

CHLORINE

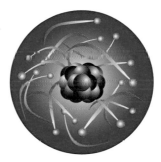

by

Jean F. Blashfield

RAINTREE
STECK-VAUGHN
PUBLISHERS

A Harcourt Company

Austin   New York
www.raintreesteckvaughn.com

Special thanks to our technical consultant,
Philip T. Johns, Ph.D.
University of Wisconsin—Whitewater, Wisconsin

Development: Books Two, Inc., Delavan, Wisconsin
        Graphics: Krueger Graphics, Janesville, Wisconsin
        Interior Design: Peg Esposito
        Photo Research: Margie Benson
        Indexing: Winston E. Black

Raintree Steck-Vaughn Publisher's Staff:
        Publishing Director: Walter Kossmann   Project Editor: Sean Dolan
        Design Manager: Richard A. Johnson

Library of Congress Cataloging-in-Publication Data:

Blashfield, Jean F.
    Chlorine / by Jean F. Blashfield.
       p. cm. — (Sparks of life)
    Includes bibliographical references and index.
    ISBN 0-7398-4358-3
       1. Chlorine--Juvenile literature. 2. Chlorine--Physiological aspects--Juvenile literature. [1. Chlorine.] I. Title.

    QD181.C5 B58 2001
    546'.732--dc21   2001019556

PHOTO CREDITS: Archive Photo 10; ©Argus Fotozrchiv/Peter Arnold, Inc. 32; B.I.F.C. cover; ©Lester V. Bergman/CORBIS 22; Bethlehem Steel 39; ©Bettmann/CORBIS 30; 42; ©Martyn F. Chillmaid/Science Photo Library 9; Dow Chemical 32; Frontier Pharmaceutical 21; ©1992 Mark Gibson/Visuals Unlimited 29; ©Adam Hart-Davis/Science Photo Library 49; ©Eric Hausman/CORBIS 52; JLM Visuals 55; ©L. Kiff/Visuals Unlimited 44; NASA 50; ©Ervin C. "Bud" Nielsen/Visuals Unlimited 16; ©Rich Poley/Visuals Unlimited 18; ©Harry J. Przekop, Stock Shop/Medichrome cover, ©James Prince/Photo Researchers 46; ©Hugh Rose/Visuals Unlimited 34; ©William Saliaz/CORBIS 23; ©Larry Stepanowicz/Visuals Unlimited 25; U.S. Signa, photo no. 165-GB-9693 in the National Archives 40; USDA Agricultural Research Service 37; Wisconsin Paper Council 36; ©Peter Yates/Science Photo Library 57.

CONTENTS

Periodic Table of the Elements

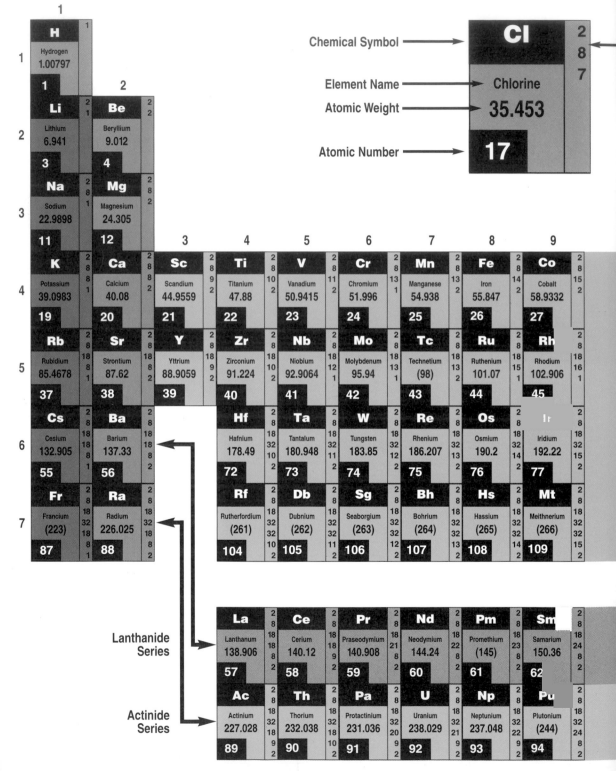

Chemical Symbol → Cl

2 8 7

Element Name → Chlorine

Atomic Weight → 35.453

Atomic Number → 17

Number of electrons in each shell, beginning with the K shell, top.

See next page for explanations.

					18
					He 2
					Helium
					4.0026

13	14	15	16	17	2
B 2,3	**C** 2,4	**N** 2,5	**O** 2,6	**F** 2,7	**Ne** 2,8
Boron	Carbon	Nitrogen	Oxygen	Fluorine	Neon
10.81	12.011	14.0067	15.9994	18.9984	20.179
5	6	7	8	9	10

13	14	15	16	17	18
Al 2,8,3	**Si** 2,8,4	**P** 2,8,5	**S** 2,8,6	**Cl** 2,8,7	**Ar** 2,8,8
Aluminum	Silicon	Phosphorus	Sulfur	Chlorine	Argon
26.9815	28.0855	30.9738	32.06	35.453	39.948
13	14	15	16	17	18

10	11	12	13	14	15	16	17	18
Ni 2,8,16,2	**Cu** 2,8,18,1	**Zn** 2,8,18,2	**Ga** 2,8,18,3	**Ge** 2,8,18,4	**As** 2,8,18,5	**Se** 2,8,18,6	**Br** 2,8,18,7	**Kr** 2,8,18,8
Nickel	Copper	Zinc	Gallium	Germanium	Arsenic	Selenium	Bromine	Krypton
58.69	63.546	65.39	69.72	72.59	74.9216	78.96	79.904	83.80
28	29	30	31	32	33	34	35	36

Pd 2,8,18,18	**Ag** 2,8,18,18,1	**Cd** 2,8,18,18,2	**In** 2,8,18,18,3	**Sn** 2,8,18,18,4	**Sb** 2,8,18,18,5	**Te** 2,8,18,18,6	**I** 2,8,18,18,7	**Xe** 2,8,18,18,8
Palladium	Silver	Cadmium	Indium	Tin	Antimony	Tellurium	Iodine	Xenon
106.42	107.868	112.41	114.82	118.71	121.75	127.6	126.905	131.29
46	47	48	49	50	51	52	53	54

Pt 2,8,18,32,17	**Au** 2,8,18,32,18	**Hg** 2,8,18,32,18	**Tl** 2,8,18,32,18	**Pb** 2,8,18,32,18	**Bi** 2,8,18,32,18	**Po** 2,8,18,32,18	**At** 2,8,18,32,18	**Rn** 2,8,18,32,18
Platinum	Gold	Mercury	Thallium	Lead	Bismuth	Polonium	Astatine	Radon
195.08	196.967	200.59	204.383	207.2	208.98	(209)	(210)	(222)
78	79	80	81	82	83	84	85	86

(Uun) 2,8,18,32,32,17,1	**(Unu)** 2,8,18,32,32,18,1	**(Uub)** 2,8,18,32,32,18,2
(Unnunilium)	(Unununium)	(Ununbium)
(269)	(272)	(277)
110	111	112

Alkali Metals	Transition Metals	Nonmetals	Metalloids	Lanthanide Series
Alkaline Earth Metals	Other Metals	Noble Gases	Actinide Series	COLOR KEYS

Eu 2,8,18,25,8,2	**Gd** 2,8,18,25,9,2	**Tb** 2,8,18,27,8,2	**Dy** 2,8,18,28,8,2	**Ho** 2,8,18,29,8,2	**Er** 2,8,18,30,8,2	**Tm** 2,8,18,31,8,2	**Yb** 2,8,18,32,8,2	**Lu** 2,8,18,32,9,2
Europium	Gadolinium	Terbium	Dysprosium	Holmium	Erbium	Thulium	Ytterbium	Lutetium
151.96	157.25	158.925	162.50	164.93	167.26	168.934	173.04	174.967
63	64	65	66	67	68	69	70	71

Am 2,8,18,32,25,8,2	**Cm** 2,8,18,32,25,9,2	**Bk** 2,8,18,32,26,9,2	**Cf** 2,8,18,32,28,8,2	**Es** 2,8,18,32,29,8,2	**Fm** 2,8,18,32,30,8,2	**Md** 2,8,18,32,31,8,2	**No** 2,8,18,32,32,8,2	**Lr** 2,8,18,32,32,9,2
Americium	Curium	Berkelium	Californium	Einsteinium	Fermium	Mendelevium	Nobelium	Lawrencium
(243)	(247)	(247)	(251)	(254)	(257)	(258)	(259)	(260)
95	96	97	98	99	100	101	102	103

A Guide to the Periodic Table

Chemical Symbol →	**Cl**	2	← Number of electrons
Element Name →	Chlorine	8	in each shell
Atomic Weight →	**35.453**	7	
Atomic Number →	**17**		

Symbol = an abbreviation of an element name, agreed on by members of the International Union of Pure and Applied Chemistry. The idea to use symbols was started by a Swedish chemist, Jöns Jakob Berzelius, about 1814. Note that the elements with numbers 110, 111, and 112, which were "discovered" in 1996, have not yet been given official names.

Atomic number = the number of protons (particles with a positive electrical charge) in the nucleus of an atom of an element; also equal to the number of electrons (particles with a negative electrical charge) found in the shells, or rings, of an atom that does not have an electrical charge.

Atomic weight = the weight of an element compared to carbon. When the Periodic Table was first developed, hydrogen was used as the standard. It was given an atomic weight of 1, but that created some difficulties, and in 1962, the standard was changed to carbon-12, which is the most common form of the element carbon, with an atomic weight of 12.

The Periodic Table on pages 4 and 5 shows the atomic weight of carbon as 12.011 because an atomic weight is an average of the weights, or masses, of all the different naturally occurring forms of an atom. Each form, called an isotope, has a different number of neutrons (uncharged particles) in the nucleus. Most elements have several isotopes, but chemists assume that any two samples of an element are made up of the same mixture of isotopes and thus have the same mass, or weight.

Electron shells = regions surrounding the nucleus of an atom in which the electrons move. Historically, electron shells have been described as orbits similar to a planet's orbit. But actually they are whole areas of a specific energy level, in which certain electrons vibrate and move around. The shell closest to the nucleus, the K shell, can contain only 2 electrons. The K shell has the lowest energy level, and it is very hard to break its electrons away. The second shell, L, can contain only 8 electrons. Others may contain up to 32 electrons. The outer shell, in which chemical reactions occur, is called the valence shell.

Periods = horizontal rows of elements in the Periodic Table. A period contains all the elements with the same number of orbital shells of electrons. Note that the actinide and lanthanide (or rare earth) elements shown in rows below the main table really belong within the table, but it is not regarded as practical to print such a wide table as would be required.

Groups = vertical columns of elements in the Periodic Table; also called families. A group contains all elements that naturally have the same number of electrons in the outermost shell or orbital of the atom. Elements in a group tend to behave in similar ways.

Group 1 = alkali metals: very reactive and so never found in nature in their pure form. Bright, soft metals, they have one valence electron and, like all metals, conduct both electricity and heat.

Group 2 = alkaline earth metals: also very reactive and thus don't occur pure in nature. Harder and denser than alkali metals, they have two valence electrons that easily combine with other chemicals.

Groups 3–12 = transition metals: the great mass of metals, with a variable number of electrons; can exist in pure form.

Groups 13–17 = transition metals, metalloids, and nonmetals. Metalloids possess some characteristics of metals and some of nonmetals. Unlike metals and metalloids, nonmetals do not conduct electricity.

Group 18 = noble, or rare, gases: in general, these nonmetallic gaseous elements do not react with other elements because their valence shells are full.

THE TWO-SIDED ELEMENT

Chlorine is one of the most useful chemical elements. For more than 150 years, it has been one of humanity's best allies in the fight against disease. But chlorine has a dark side, too. It is useful, but it also plays a vital role in chemicals that harm living things and the environment.

Chlorine is an element, a substance that cannot be broken down further without changing its character. This element has been given the symbol Cl. When chlorine binds with most other substances, especially those that do not contain carbon (C, element #6), it is incredibly useful—and quite safe. But when chlorine joins with carbon-containing compounds, it can become a substance that is terribly destructive to our environment and our bodies.

There's no way to avoid chlorine. It's

all around us, in the food we eat, in the objects we use, and even in our bodies. Sometimes its presence occurs naturally. Other times, it is the result of human activities. You wouldn't want to avoid chlorine, anyway. We need a certain amount in our food to stay healthy. In addition, it kills harmful bacteria in the water we drink and the pools in which we swim.

The Greenish-Yellow Gas

In 1774, Carl Wilhelm Scheele, a chemist in Sweden, studied pyrolusite, which is the main ore of the metallic element manganese (Mn, element #25). He soaked the mineral in a powerful chemical called hydrochloric acid, which is written HCl (hydrogen is H, element #1). He was astonished to see—and smell—a foul-smelling, colorful gas bubbling up from the acid. He recorded what he observed and called the gas *chlorine* for the Greek word *chloros*, which means "greenish-yellow." Then Scheele paid no more attention to the odd gas.

Chlorine gas

Because Scheele recorded the discovery of the gas and named it, he is often credited with discovering chlorine, but he made no attempt to identify it as an element. He is known for the discovery of a number of elements, especially oxygen (O, element #8), but chlorine isn't one of them. Scheele died young because he had a bad habit of tasting the chemicals he worked with.

A few years after Scheele's discovery, Count Claude-Louis Berthollet, a French-Italian chemist, demonstrated that the gas could be used as a bleach to remove color from fabric. Soon, and for the first time, people were wearing truly white clothing. However, Berthollet still thought the gas was an oxygen-containing compound rather than an element.

The discovery of chlorine as an element did not occur until 1810 with the work of English chemist Sir Humphry Davy, who

Sir Humphry Davy

had already discovered several chemical elements. Davy was so famous as a science lecturer in London that crowds often came to listen to him and watch his fascinating demonstrations.

One of the demonstrations they found most fascinating was electrolysis. This is the process of putting an electric current through a fluid containing a substance in order to analyze it. The electricity would cause fluids to break apart, or decompose, into the elements of which they were composed. In this way, Davy demonstrated that the gas that bubbled up when he put a metal in hydrochloric acid was, in fact, a gaseous element.

One of the members of Davy's enthusiastic audience was young Michael Faraday, who later became Davy's assistant. Faraday eventually developed a way to use force, or pressure, to change chlorine gas into a liquid. It was later found that chlorine can also be turned into solid pale-yellow crystals by reducing its temperature to −103°C (−153°F), just below its freezing point.

The Reactive Element

Unlike many other elements, chlorine atoms cannot be observed in nature. They don't exist individually, except once in a while in the hot gases spewing out of volcanoes. This absence of atomic chlorine in nature is due to the structure of chlorine atoms.

Chlorine has atomic number 17. This means that it has 17 protons, or positively charged particles, in its nucleus. It also has 17 electrons, or negatively charged particles, in orbit around the nucleus.

Electrons exist in certain orbits, or shells, by a specific pattern. In the Periodic Table of the Elements (pages 4 and 5), chlorine is in Period 3, the third horizontal row. All the elements in this period have three electron shells. Two electrons move in the first, or inner shell, and eight in the second. Chlorine's third, or outer, shell, also called the valence shell, has seven electrons $(2 + 8 + 7 = 17)$.

With seven electrons in the outer shell, chlorine is like the other elements in the group, or vertical column, labeled 17 (also called (Group VIIA) in the Periodic Table. Other elements in the group, called halogens, include fluorine (F, element #9), bromine (Br, #35), iodine (I, #53), and astatine (At, #85). They all react very easily with other elements, especially metals.

Atoms are stable, or non-reacting, when they have eight electrons in that valence shell, so chlorine atoms want to bond with any electron they can find to complete that valence shell and become stable. They do this by taking an electron from another atom or by sharing an electron with another atom.

To exist at all, pure chlorine gas needs to share an electron with another chlorine atom. The gas exists as a two-atom, or diatomic, molecule, which is written Cl_2. Oxygen in the air we breathe is also a diatomic molecule, O_2. Sir Humphry Davy discovered that chlorine behaves like oxygen. The diatomic molecules of both elements readily split and link up with atoms of other elements.

Diatomic chlorine is more than 2.5 times heavier than air. When released into the atmosphere, it tends to linger in a cloud near the ground. This is one of the reasons that a leak of chlorine gas can be dangerous.

The pungent odor of chlorine in air can be smelled at as little as three parts

A diatomic chlorine molecule, Cl_2

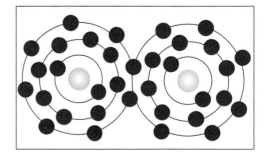

per million (ppm). At only five times that amount—15 ppm—many people's throats become irritated. A person taking only a few deep breaths in air containing 1,000 ppm chlorine is likely to die very quickly. Obviously, industrial workers handling chlorine must be very careful. Workers handling chlorine containers must wear gas masks to protect themselves.

Chlorine's Isotopes

Natural diatomic chlorine is actually a combination of two different forms, or isotopes, of the element. An element may have several different isotopes when its atoms vary in the number of neutrons, or uncharged particles, in the nucleus. These forms all exist in the same place in the Periodic Table (*isotope* means "same place").

All chlorine atoms have 17 protons, or positively charged particles, in the nucleus. They are balanced electrically by 17 electrons in orbit around the nucleus. However, about three-quarters of natural chlorine has 18 neutrons in the nucleus and is identified as the isotope chlorine-35 (17 electrons and 18 neutrons make Cl-35). The other quarter is Cl-37, which has 20 neutrons in the nucleus. This fact was discovered by English physicist Francis Aston in 1920. For this and similar work with the mass spectroscope, the measuring device he invented, Aston won the 1922 Nobel Prize in chemistry.

Many other chlorine isotopes are made artificially. They are all radioactive, meaning that they give off high-energy particles. The most significant artificial isotope is Cl-36. It is produced when potassium chloride is treated with radiation. (Potassium is K, for *kalium,* element #19.)

Busy Ions

Sodium (Na, for the Latin *natrium*, element #11) is a silvery, very soft metal. Chlorine is a poisonous greenish gas. When the

Chlorine ions (in green) and sodium ions (in silver) are held together in ionic bonds that make all salt crystals cubic in shape.

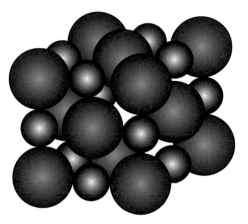

two are put together, the metal reacts with the gas. A yellowish cloud forms that, when condensed, crystallizes into white, non-poisonous, common table salt, or sodium chloride, NaCl.

That is what is seen in the laboratory, at the visible level. However, inside the elements themselves, at the atomic level, things look very different. The sodium atoms give up an electron to the chlorine atoms. Both elements are then ions, which are atoms (or molecules—groups of atoms attached to each other) with an electrical charge. The sodium atoms have given up electrons and become positive ions, written Na^+. They now have more positive protons than negative electrons. The chlorine atoms have taken on sodium's released electrons and become negative ions, written Cl^-. They now have more negative electrons than positive protons.

The two kinds of ions are held together by the attraction that a negative charge and a positive charge have for each other. This attraction is called an ionic bond. The positive and negative ions alternate in a cubic structure that is a salt crystal.

The creation of table salt—NaCl—out of two very different elements is an example of a redox reaction. *Redox* stands for "reduction" and "oxidation." It sounds as if an oxidation reaction involves the element oxygen, but that is not necessarily the case. It only needs to involve the release of an electron, yielding a positive ion of sodium. That electron is taken up by the chlorine atom, yielding a negative ion—that is the reduction process.

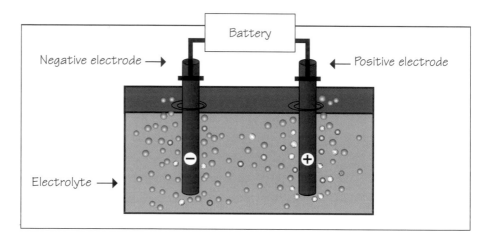

This type of simple but clever electrolysis equipment was used by Humphry Davy to isolate chlorine and other chemical elements.

Ionic bonds are easily broken. When salt is dissolved in water, separate positive sodium ions and negative chlorine ions are produced. If an electric charge is put through the water, the ions react to it, flowing toward the appropriate part of the apparatus. The negative chlorine ions (called anions) move toward the positive pole, or anode. This is the electrolysis process that Davy carried out. The chlorine bubbled up as diatomic gas.

Actually, when sodium chloride is decomposed by electrolysis, the process is not quite so simple and direct. Instead, it produces chloride gas at the anode and hydrogen at the cathode, or negative pole. This is because the electricity actually acts on both the salt and the water it is dissolved in. The water molecule, H_2O, breaks down into hydrogen gas, which is diatomic, H_2, and a hydroxide ion, OH^-. That ion then combines with the sodium left over from the sodium chloride to make sodium hydroxide, NaOH.

$$2NaCl + 2H_2O \rightarrow Cl_2 + H_2 + 2OH^- + 2Na^+$$

$$2OH^- + 2Na^+ \rightarrow 2NaOH$$

Where Chlorine is Found

Chlorine is the twentieth most abundant element on Earth, though it is rarely found as a free element. The only time the gaseous element is found free is in the spewing gases of some volcanoes. Even there, though, it is more likely to be found as hydrogen chloride, HCl. However, the great heat sometimes breaks apart the hydrogen chloride molecules.

Chlorine exists most often on Earth as an anion called chloride, Cl^-. Chloride ions combine readily with such metallic positive ions, or cations, as sodium, potassium, iron (Fe, for *ferrum*, element #26), aluminum (Al, #13), and magnesium (Mg, #12).

Sodium chloride, or table salt, is made up of equal numbers of sodium and chlorine ions. Potassium chloride, KCl, is very similar to sodium chloride. Like sodium, potassium atoms have one electron in the valence shell to give away, so one potassium atom balances one chlorine atom. On the other hand, magnesium chloride is made up of one magnesium ion and two chloride ions. This is because magnesium has two valence electrons that it can give away to chlorine atoms in order to form an electrically neutral molecule. Magnesium chloride is written $MgCl_2$. Sodium, potassium, and magnesium chlorides are all found naturally in seawater.

Chlorine also combines readily with substances that contain carbon, which are called organic substances. These chemicals

In Thailand, salt is obtained by letting seawater into shallow ponds, where it evaporates, leaving salt that quickly dries.

are referred to as organochlorines. Today, organochlorines have a bad reputation because some of them are carcinogenic, or cancer-causing, and harmful to the environment. However, organochlorines have always played a part in human life.

Finding Uses

For hundreds of years, woven cotton fabric had been bleached by wetting it with sour milk and placing it in the sun. But this was no longer practical in the 18th century, when huge, automated looms of textile factories started turning out miles of cotton fabric. Toward the end of the eighteenth century, it was discovered that a solution of chlorine (though it had not yet been identified as an element) would do the job, regardless of the weather.

In 19th-century England, one of the most important industrial processes was the making of soap. Throughout most of history, soap has been made by combining animal fat with a very alkaline (nonacidic) chemical, usually sodium hydroxide, NaOH. The soap industry required the processing of seawater to obtain sodium for making sodium hydroxide. But the process released an unwanted by-product into the air. That by-product was hydrochloric acid, HCl. The people in nearby farms and towns were not happy with the result because the acid in the air harmed their crops and homes. The first air-pollution laws were passed, requiring that the acid not be released into the air. Instead, it was trapped in large vats. The trapped hydrochloric acid became a source of chlorine for use in making bleaching powder.

Chlorine found its first truly important use as a bacteria-killer in drinking water. This began in the 1890s. Since then, it has been used for this purpose almost everywhere around the world. Even people who drink water directly from their own well generally have a means of adding chlorine to it. Apparently, the chemical causes the proteins in bacteria to disintegrate, which kills them.

Throughout the twentieth century, the number of uses for chlorine has greatly increased. What has also increased, though, is the number of health and environmental problems related to the greenish-yellow element.

The Meaning of "Green"

It seems as if the words *chlorine* and *chlorophyll* ought to be related. They are, but in a way that has nothing to do with chlorine being present in chlorophyll. The word *chlorine,* as we saw, is derived from the Greek *chloros,* meaning "greenish-yellow." In the word *chlorophyll,* the *chlor–* refers to the color green. Chlorophyll is the coloring matter, or pigment, that makes most plants green.

For higher animals, chlorine is a macronutrient, meaning that it is an element needed in fairly large amounts to sustain life. But for plants, it's a micronutrient—only small amounts are needed. However, those small amounts can be important.

Chlorine—as the chloride ion—works in plant tissue to enable cells to hold water. Without sufficient chloride, plants shrivel up. Their leaves begin to rot, turning brown in spots. In general, most soils contain enough chloride for the needs of any plants.

THE GIFT OF SAFE WATER

The addition of chlorine to drinking water takes place at both small private wells and major metropolitan waterworks.

Over the centuries, millions of people have been killed by diseases that were carried in or spread by polluted water. These deaths were most often the result of harmful bacteria that caused such diseases as cholera and typhoid fever. Even today, especially in the poorer nations of the world, cholera is a major cause of death.

The fact that bacteria caused disease was not fully realized until the late nineteenth century, but the importance of that discovery was limited without access to a reliable way of killing the bacteria. Chlorine turned out to be the answer.

In 2000, *Life* magazine listed the addition of chlorine to drinking water as one of the most important inventions of the past thousand years. Using chlorine in this way has saved an uncountable number of human lives.

Disinfecting Our Water

Cholera is a disease that causes terrible diarrhea. If not successfully treated, the victim loses so much body fluid that he or she dies. Cholera outbreaks are still common today in places where natural disasters have occurred and bodies of dead humans and animals are allowed to rot in water supplies.

Typhoid fever, which is also caused by a specific type of bacteria that gets into water supplies, causes the victim to develop a dangerously high temperature and suffer many other painful symptoms. Until the medicines called antibiotics were invented, typhoid was often fatal.

In the 1880s, Dr. John Snow proposed that an ongoing cholera epidemic in London originated in a well that had been contaminated. It was not until a typhoid epidemic in 1897, though, that chlorine was first used to kill bacteria in water. Within a very short time, all drinking water in Britain was being treated with chlorine. The rest of the industrial world followed.

In the United States, chlorine was first added to the water supply in Jersey City, New Jersey, in 1908. Other cities quickly followed New Jersey's lead. Throughout the country, the death rate from typhoid dropped from 36 cases per 100,000 people in 1900 to only 5 per 100,000 in 1928. This wonderful change was a direct result of the chlorination of drinking water.

The United States and other developed countries have benefited from chlorination, but not all countries, especially those that are poor, have been as fortunate. The World Health Organization estimates that 25,000 people still die every day of diseases carried by water that is not adequately disinfected.

How Chlorine Works

In purifying water, chlorine is used at two different times. It's used first when water from a natural source is being prepared for use as drinking water. It is used again when sewage, or waste-water, that has been used is being cleaned to be returned to the natural source.

The reaction of chlorine in water releases three kinds of ions, as follows:

$$Cl_2 + H_2O \rightarrow 2H^+ + OCl^- + Cl^-$$

Chlorine + water → hydrogen ions + hypochlorite ions + chloride ions

The hypochlorite ion kills bacteria by the chemical process of oxidation. The chemical substances, especially proteins, that make up the bacteria lose electrons to the hypochlorite in the water. That loss kills them.

After natural disasters, emergency relief workers often provide chlorine tablets or other chemicals for purifying wells and other sources of water. Even so, the devastation of earthquakes and hurricanes is often made worse by cholera and typhoid epidemics that develop before water supplies can be repaired.

After Drinking

Chlorine is also added at the other end of the cycle, when waste water, having been used, must be treated before being returned to the source. First, any solid material is allowed to settle out. Then the waste water is filtered. Finally, chlorine is added to kill bacteria.

However, waste water, after being processed this way, cannot be sent directly back into the ground while it still contains the chlorine used to disinfect it. The chlorine could harm the environment. Sulfur dioxide, SO_2, is added to remove the chlorine as sulfur chloride. (Sulfur is S, element #16.)

Unfortunately, small amounts of chlorine often still remain in water that is pumped back into a lake or the ground. Any organic (carbon-containing) compounds in the water may be converted into organochlorine compounds. Some scientists regard such compounds as dangerous because a few have been found to be carcinogenic, or cancer-causing. But probably no U.S. water sources contain more than 50 parts per billion of organochlorine compounds. That amount is only half the level set by the Environmental Protection Administration (EPA) for safe drinking water.

Using Other Chemicals

Although the amount of organochlorines that may be in our drinking water is tiny, many municipal water supplies around the world are beginning to use ozone instead of chlorine to disinfect water. Ozone is a three-atom, or triatomic, molecule of oxygen. Although it is more expensive than chlorine, ozone has the advantage of killing viruses as well as bacteria. It can prevent more diseases than can chlorine, which kills only bacteria.

Another chemical that often replaces pure chlorine in water purification is chlorine dioxide, ClO_2. Humphry Davy discovered chlorine dioxide quite early in his chemical investigations when he reacted potassium chlorate, $KClO_3$, with sulfuric acid, H_2SO_4.

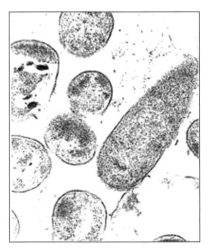

Chlorine dioxide breaks down the cell walls of these bacteria, seen through a microscope. Shown here: before application of ClO_2 (left) and after (right).

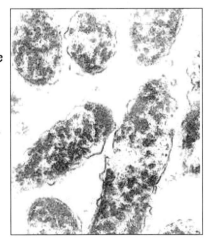

First used for water purification in Belgium, chlorine dioxide is used more widely in Europe than in the United States. Its major advantage over chlorine is that it remains a gas when introduced into water, whereas chlorine reacts with water.

The disadvantage of chlorine dioxide is that it cannot be shipped under pressure. When pressure is applied, the gas explodes. Therefore, it has to be produced where it is to be used. It is generally produced by mixing sodium chlorate, $NaClO_3$, with hydrogen peroxide, H_2O_2, and sulfuric acid, H_2SO_4.

Chlorine dioxide is used widely in a variety of industries where microbes, or microscopic organisms, can easily grow. Equipment and rooms must be regularly cleaned with a chemical that stops microbe growth. Such industries include the dairy and beef-processing industries, beverage-making industries, paper and pulp industries—all industries involving materials that originated as living things.

Since the 1930s, another form of chlorine, called chloramine, has been used increasingly by water-supply authorities. Chloramine compounds are made by combining chlorine and ammonia, NH_3. Any of three compounds may result—monochloramine (NH_2Cl), dichloramine ($NHCl_2$), or nitrogen trichloride (NCl_3).

Chloramines were first used before World War II (1939–1945) to disinfect water because they made the water taste and smell better than it did with diatomic chlorine. Then it was found that chloramines have an advantage in that they continue to act for longer than plain chlorine does. However, ammonia for making chloramines was unavailable during World War II. Public waterworks returned to using pure chlorine. Most have

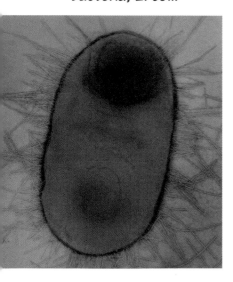

Chlorine compounds are used to kill bacteria, seen here greatly enlarged through a microscope. This is the common stomach bacteria, E. coli.

continued to do so since that time.

A problem with using chlorine in public water supplies is that it tends to produce such by-products as chloroform, which is carcinogenic. Chloramines are less likely than pure chlorine to react with organic materials in the water and produce chloroform or similar compounds. Some people believe that any possible bad effects of chloramines can be offset by taking vitamin C. However, there is no strong evidence that this works.

The water used in swimming pools must be treated frequently with chlorine to keep disease-causing bacteria from spoiling the fun.

Pools and the Problems of Swimmers

Chlorine is added to the water in swimming pools for the same reason it is put in drinking water—prevention of disease. It is usually added in the form of sodium hypochloride, $NaOCl$, or calcium hypochlorite, $Ca(OCl)_2$.

Sometimes people say, "There's too much chlorine in this pool" when their eyes start to burn. However, if the water is just allowed to sit for a while, the excess chlorine will drift into the atmosphere, leaving the pool water just right. It is not actually the chlorine that makes the swimmer's eyes hurt. Instead, it's the acidity of the water.

Whether used in water supplies or swimming pools, chlorine makes water more acid—it lowers the pH number. The pH number is a measure of the acidity or alkalinity of a substance on a scale of 0 to 14. A lower number means the substance is more acid. A higher number means that it is alkaline, or basic. Neutrality is in the middle, at 7.

A substance is an acid when it produces hydrogen ions when dissolved in water. As we saw, the addition of chlorine to water releases hydrogen ions. The presence of these ions in water is likely to irritate the sensitive mucous membranes around the eyes.

People who swim a lot often have their hair turn lighter in color. That is because the chlorine added to pool water also acts as a bleach. It lightens the color and dehydrates (removes water) from the hair shaft. A dried hair shaft is more prone to damage from chemicals. People who swim frequently should rinse chlorine out of their hair right after swimming. Then they should use a shampoo that neutralizes chlorine's acidic properties.

Another problem for frequent swimmers is dry skin. It occurs because water breaks down the skin's protective outer layer, allowing moisture to escape more easily. Chlorine accelerates this process. Taking a shower immediately after swimming in a pool will help.

Salt and Water

Humans add chlorine as Cl_2 to freshwater to purify the water for drinking, but chlorine exists naturally in all water sources, especially the sea, as chloride ions, Cl^-. Water naturally contains many other chemicals besides H_2O molecules. These other substances come from minerals in rocks and soil that are dissolved by rainwater and carried into rivers and then into the ocean. They exist in small amounts in freshwater but in great amounts in the sea.

About 2.5 percent of seawater consists of minerals in the form of ions, especially sodium (Na^+) and chloride (Cl^-). In weight, there is about twice the chloride in seawater as there is sodium, but chlorine is a heavier element than sodium. Seawater also contains other ions, such as sulfate (SO_2^{4-}), magnesium (Mg^{2+}), calcium (Ca^{2+}), and potassium (K^+).

CHLORIDE FOR LIFE

Sodium and chlorine, which make up common table salt, share the position of being the ninth most common elements in the human body. Life began in the salty oceans, and living things still require salt to live.

The importance of salt, both for the taste of food and for human health, has been known since ancient times when some people were paid in salt. Our word *salary*, meaning the wages a person receives for working, comes from the ancient Latin for "salt."

The Chloride Ion

It seems odd that an element that is described as a poisonous gas should be an important element in the human body. But chlorine does not exist in the body as chlorine atoms or even as diatomic chlorine molecules. When salt enters our bodies, it is dissolved in water and separates into sodium ions and

Crystals of sodium chloride, called table salt

chloride ions. Chloride, Cl⁻, behaves very differently in living things than chlorine, Cl_2, does.

Ions in the body are called electrolytes. The flow of electrons is electricity, so ions can be said to transmit electrical signals in the body. Such signals are carried by sodium, potassium, and chloride ions. All three of these electrolytes are free to move in the fluid that continually bathes cells, both inside and out.

Electrical signals consist of changes in the concentration of ions. In muscles, for example, ions tell muscle tissue to contract. The transmission of a message along a nerve cell is carried out by ion flow, creating electrical balance.

All three of these electrolytes—chloride, sodium, and potassium—are necessary in the proper amounts for the body to function correctly. Too much or too little of any of them, or even the lack of a proper balance between them, can have serious consequences for bodily function and health.

For every 1 kilogram (2.2 pounds) of body weight in a human, about 1.5 grams (about 0.5 ounce) consists of chloride ions. They are found in the blood that flows throughout the body, but they are also concentrated in the digestive secretions in the stomach and in the fluid that runs through the spinal cord.

Chloride in the Blood

Respiration is the taking in of oxygen and the release of carbon dioxide. We often think of it as something that our lungs do, when they take oxygen from the air and send it through the bloodstream into every cell of the body. But respiration actually occurs in the cells. Each cell takes in oxygen, uses it to burn food for the energy to carry out its various functions, and then releases carbon dioxide. The red blood cells then gather up the carbon dioxide from throughout the body and return it to the lungs, where it is exhaled into the air.

The chloride ion plays an essential role in the respiration

process. Part of the process of oxygen being carried in the red blood cells requires the temporary formation of bicarbonate ions, HCO_3^-. These ions leave the red blood cells and flow into the plasma, which is the fluid that holds the red and white blood cells. To offset this flow of negative bicarbonate ions out of the blood cells, chloride ions flow in. The reverse process happens when carbon dioxide is taken from the cells to the lungs. This process is called the chloride shift.

An Acid in the Stomach

An acid is a chemical that gives up hydrogen ions when dissolved in a liquid such as water. Sometimes called muriatic acid when used in industry, hydrochloric acid is the simplest acid, HCl. Yet it is also one of the strongest acids.

Hydrochloric acid is used by industry to eat away unwanted coatings on metal, and it can burn the skin. Yet it it is also found in our stomach, where it plays a vital role in digestion. About one-half of 1 percent of the volume of the digestive juices in our stomachs is hydrochloric acid.

Why doesn't hydrochloric acid eat away our stomachs? That mystery baffled scientists for a while. Then they discovered that the lining of the stomach also secretes a thick protective coating, called mucus, that does not react with the acid.

Hydrochloric acid mixes with a chemical secreted by the stomach to form pepsin, the enzyme in gastric fluids that digests

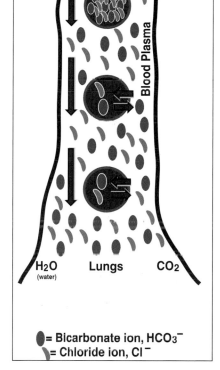

$$CO_2 + H_2O \rightleftharpoons HCO_3^- + H^+$$
(from cells)   (water in blood)   (bicarbonate ion)   (hydrogen ion)

Blood Plasma

H_2O (water)   Lungs CO_2

● = Bicarbonate ion, HCO_3^-
〰 = Chloride ion, Cl^-

The chloride shift in blood

the nutrients called proteins. Pepsin works only in the presence of hydrochloric acid. Without enough acid, food is not digested properly. Acid is neutralized as food enters the small intestine.

Perhaps more important than its role in digestion is the work hydrochloric acid does in keeping germs from entering the body. The acidic environment of the stomach acts as a disinfectant that kills disease-causing bacteria that might enter on food.

Sometimes, though, people have too much acid in their stomachs. This is a condition called hyperacidity. A person who is under a lot of stress, or eating the wrong foods, or suffering from various other conditions may have too much acid in the stomach. Then it sometimes backs up into the esophagus, the tube between the throat and the stomach, where there is no mucus coating. A person may notice this as a discomfort that is often called heartburn, though nothing is really burning and it has nothing to do with the heart.

Heartburn can be treated by swallowing an antacid, something that counteracts the acid. One common kind of antacid contains calcium carbonate, $CaCO_3$. The carbonate reacts with the HCl, producing harmless water and carbon dioxide.

Blood, Sweat, and Urine

Every part of our body, down to the tiniest cell, is bathed in water. We get rid of some water through urination and sweating. We must replace it by drinking more water.

Sometimes, though, electrolytes do not work right, and our bodies retain fluid. Medicines called diuretics make the body release fluids as urine. Diuretics are commonly given to people with high blood pressure, a condition called hypertension. It means that the heart is having to pump with more force to move the blood through the arteries than is healthy for the person. By taking a diuretic medicine, a person allows fluid to leave the body, and his or her heart does not have to work so hard.

This young girl's face is puffy with edema, which is the accumulation of fluids in the body.

An even larger amount of chloride ions can be lost from the body through excessive sweating or urination. They can also be lost through a spate of vomiting. A person with a fever puts out less chloride in urine than a person with a normal temperature. A person normally releases about 10 or 12 grams (0.3 or 0.4 ounce) of chloride each day in urine.

No matter how chloride ions are lost, they need to be replaced. Chlorine, or at least chloride, is a macronutrient, one of the elements needed by humans in fairly large amounts.

Under normal conditions, it's not difficult for human beings to get enough chlorine. All it takes is salt. Nutritionists recommend that adults get no more than 3 grams (3,000 milligrams) of salt a day. This is probably only half of what most adults in the United States take in. Most processed foods contain considerable salt, and most of us add more salt to our food at the table.

A person with high blood pressure is often asked by the doctor to cut down on intake. This is because of the sodium in the salt, not the chloride. Many grocery stores now carry products that are lower in sodium than most commonly processed foods. One way a person can cut down is to flavor food with potassium chloride, KCl, instead of sodium chloride, $NaCl$. One common salt substitute is half $NaCl$ and half KCl. Strangely enough, humans need potassium more than they need sodium, because the body conserves sodium but not potassium.

Going to Sleep

In 1846, a chemical was first used to put someone to sleep for an operation. That chemical was ether. The very next year,

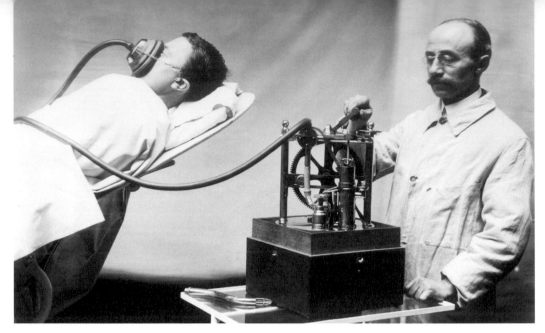

A doctor administers chloroform in this late-19th-century photograph. The amount given was controlled by turning a crank.

another new chemical was used for the same purpose. Chloroform, also called trichloromethane, $CHCl_3$, is a sweet-smelling and sweet-tasting fluid. Scottish physician James Simpson had a patient breathe the fumes. The patient slept through the surgery without feeling any pain. The public remained suspicious of this newfangled idea until a few years later when Queen Victoria of Great Britain chose to be given chloroform when she gave birth to her eighth child.

From the time of its earliest use, however, some patients had difficulty recovering from the use of chloroform. If used in the wrong amounts, it damaged their internal organs, especially the liver and kidneys. The amount needed to put a patient to sleep was alarmingly close to the amount needed to kill the person.

Chloroform is no longer used as a general anesthetic because safer compounds have been discovered. However, many of us are regularly exposed to small amounts of chloroform. It forms naturally when organic material gets into chlorinated water, for example, and thus it is often in our drinking water. For this same reason, swimming pools often give off a little chloroform. It may also form in enclosed showers or hot tubs when people stay in the hot water for a long time.

Watching Out

Chlorine can be dangerous if it gets into the body as something other than chloride ions. People who work in the chlorine industry are not supposed to be exposed to more Cl_2 than 1 part per million averaged over a 40-hour week.

Many scientists are concerned that chlorine-containing substances may play a role in the formation of cancer. They are carcinogenic. This means that they have the ability to change those parts of cells that control growth. Instead of an orderly growth of new cells to replace old ones, new cells begin growing in a wild, haphazard way, causing what is called a tumor and eventually damaging the normal tissue. Such abnormal cell growth is often one of the many serious diseases called cancer.

Some people are more concerned about the immediate damage that chlorine does to humans by irritating the mucous membranes. These are the sensitive tissues in the eyes, nose, throat, and lungs that secrete moisturizing fluids. In people who have asthma, breathing large quantities of chlorine gas can cause immediate closing of the breathing passages. In everyone, it can cause a serious condition called pulmonary edema in which lung tissue swells and the person has trouble breathing.

Chlorine is one of the substances of modern life that scientists argue about frequently. Does it cause serious damage to the body or doesn't it? Does it actually cause cancer or just encourage its growth once the disease is present? Or does it actually initiate the formation of cancers? Does the fact that it is stored in body fat mean that people should stay thin if at all possible? These arguments will probably continue for a long time, especially as long as chlorine is a useful chemical in industry.

THE INDUSTRIAL CHEMICAL

Since chlorine, Cl_2, does not exist naturally, it must be produced. It is produced easily, by the electrolysis of saltwater. Salt was first separated into its elements by electrolysis in 1800. The same process is used today on a much bigger scale.

Brine is fluid salt, found in large deposits throughout the world. The salt in these deposits collected when ancient seas covered the land. As they retreated, they left behind massive quantities of sodium chloride. Sometimes the salt dried and became rock salt, also called halite, which is mined. Not all of these deposits dried into deposits of white crystals, however. Instead, some pockets of salt held water, making a mushy fluid called brine. Brine can just be pumped out of the ground.

This huge industrial machine, called Chlorine II, produces Cl_2 by the electrolysis of brine.

Electrolysis of Salt

The electrolysis of brine produces two chemicals needed by industry: chlorine gas and sodium hydroxide, or caustic soda, also called lye. It also produces hydrogen gas.

$$2NaCl + 2H_2O \rightarrow Cl_2 + 2NaOH + H_2$$

salt + water $\rightarrow$ chlorine gas + sodium hydroxide + hydrogen gas

It wasn't until the 1890s that electrolysis moved out of the laboratory and into the factory. This happened when electric power in large quantities became available. Suddenly chlorine became available as a raw material for other processes, and it has been increasingly present in industry and the environment ever since.

The chlorine gas produced by electrolysis is actually mixed with considerable water vapor. The gas is sent into cooling chambers where the water vapor condenses out. The final product must be stored in containers made of stone, glass, or rubber, which cannot be eaten away, or corroded, by chlorine.

Numerous products—seemingly unrelated items—have something in common: chlorine plays a role in their manufacture. Such products are as varied as cosmetics and computers, paperback books and toothpaste. It is estimated that at least 85 percent of all medicines and drug products are made with processes involving chlorine.

Every year, the amount of chlorine produced in North America increases. The chlorine industry projects that by 2004, almost 14 billion kilograms (30 billion pounds) of the gas will be needed annually. Interestingly, only about 1 percent of that amount will be used for disinfecting water. About 33 percent goes into other chemicals, especially medicines, and 25 percent into plastics. Some is used in solvents (chemicals that dissolve other substances), such as dry-cleaning chemicals. And about 10

The cleanup of chlorine and related materials from an accident or waste site requires wearing safety gear.

percent of industrial chlorine is used in bleaching, especially in the paper industry.

Most chlorine has to be shipped from the electrolysis plant to various factories. Shipping itself is a dangerous business. Chlorine gas can leak during shipping, such as when a tank truck overturns or a railway car flips off the tracks and breaks open. When this happens, whole towns may need to be evacuated until the dangerous gas has dispersed into the atmosphere. Liquid chlorine runs into streams, killing fish. Fire-fighting units in most towns receive some training in how to deal with a chlorine spill or leak.

Turning Things White

One of the uses of sodium hydroxide is to produce bleach, a chemical that whitens things. Sodium hydroxide is once again combined with chlorine, this time not to produce salt again but to obtain sodium hypochlorite, NaOCl. A solution of 95 percent water and 5 percent sodium hypochlorite is the useful bleach that we use at home:

$$Cl_2 + NaOH \rightarrow NaOCl + (Cl^- + H^+ \text{ ions})$$

It wasn't easy discovering a practical bleach for household use. When chlorine gas is dissolved in water, it forms hydrochloric acid, which can eat away the fabric being bleached. The problem wasn't solved until sodium hypochlorite, NaOCl, was used. Bleaching powder, used industrially, is $Ca(OCl)_2$. In both of these chemicals, the hypochlorite ion ($ClO-$) does the actual bleaching.

Household bleach is fairly safe if it is kept out of the reach of little children. However, even if a child swallows some bleach, it is usually vomited right back up. Even so, bleach can be harmful if taken internally, and a doctor should be consulted if this happens.

The danger increases when people decide to improve the cleaning power of bleach by mixing it with liquid ammonia, NH_3. Ammonia, too, is generally safe around the house. However, when the two are mixed, the liquid releases substances called chloramines, NH_2Cl. If inhaled, chloramines can seriously damage the lungs.

Chlorine bleach cannot be used to whiten all fabrics. It damages wool and silk. Polyester and other synthetic fabrics tend to turn yellowish when exposed to chlorine bleach. Oxygen bleaches are safer for such fabrics. Chlorine bleach should never be used full strength on clothing. It needs to be diluted in water to avoid damaging the fabric.

The whitening and disinfecting power of chlorine makes it a useful ingredient in cleansing powders and other products used to keep sinks, stoves, and counters clean. Plain laundry bleach is much cheaper and just as effective as the more expensive compounds sold for disinfecting food-preparation areas at home.

In 1913, Dow Chemical, one of the early makers of chlorine bleach, stopped making bleach. The company decided to concentrate instead on finding ways to use chlorine as a raw material in other industrial processes. Many have been found.

The Paper Industry

Bleaching fabric and laundry is a minor business compared to the use of chlorine to bleach wood pulp to make white paper.

This wood pulp for use in making paper has been bleached white with sodium chlorate bleach.

Some unbleached paper has always been used, such as that used to make grocery bags, which is called kraft paper. But white paper is used much more often.

For decades, the paper industry dumped its chemical wastes into nearby rivers. The fish swimming in these rivers were poisoned. In recent years, the paper industry has solved much of this problem in two ways. They have almost eliminated these toxic substances by switching to the use of chlorine dioxide instead of plain chlorine for bleaching the pulp, and they have stopped dumping waste into rivers.

Chlorine is still used in the paper industry. Today it is used to remove the ink from paper that is being recycled. Concern for the environment is often a matter of having to choose between two potentially harmful ways of doing things. Is it better to recycle paper, which requires the removal of ink, or is it better not to recycle paper at all?

The paper industry has been looking for ways to bleach paper that do not harm the environment. It has been projected that by the year 2015, the industry may no longer use chlorine at all. In the meantime, many people support the drive of environmentalists to encourage consumers to buy tissues, napkins, and other paper items in their natural, unbleached color in order to keep chlorine out of landfills, where garbage is dumped.

Sitting on Chlorine

Chlorine gas bonds with organic (carbon-containing) matter to form organochlorines. Many plastics are organochlorine products. One of the most common is vinyl chloride, C_2H_3Cl, which is also called chloroethylene. At room temperature, vinyl chloride is a colorless, flammable gas with a slightly sweet odor. Although it had been known as a chemical for more than 100 years, it did not become truly useful until it was discovered that the molecule could react with itself. The result was a large molecule, called a polymer, made up of small repeating units—the C_2H_3Cl molecules—called monomers. This process, called polymerization, is used to make a rubber substitute, polyvinyl chloride (PVC). The manufacturing of PVC is the most common industrial use of chlorine.

PVC is used in numerous items, from fake-leather upholstery to siding for houses to raincoats. It has almost totally replaced metal in water and waste pipes in buildings. Metal pipes rust and corrode, whereas PVC pipes do not. It is estimated that the making

Fishing nets made of PVC are inexpensive and strong. The polymer material can withstand most chemicals found in ocean water.

of PVC will be the main use of chlorine well into the twenty-first century.

As useful as vinyl chloride can be, it can also seriously harm the health of people who work with it. Vinyl chloride damages nerves and can even cut off the circulation in fingertips so that they turn white.

Widespread Chemical Uses

Carbon tetrachloride (also called tetrachloromethane), CCl_4, used to be available for use at home as a spot cleaner on wool and other materials that had to be dry-cleaned. The volatile (easily evaporated) and inflammable fluid would soak into the material, dissolving the stain. When the material dried, it left a white residue that could be easily brushed off.

For generations, "carbon tet," as the chemical was popularly called, was found in virtually every home. But then the clear, sweetish-smelling liquid was found to be carcinogenic. It was taken off the market and is now used only in industries, such as in the manufacture of agricultural insecticides, paints, and other chemicals. For dry-cleaning, carbon tet has been replaced by other chemicals.

Chloroform, $CHCl_3$, once used as an anesthetic, has been used as an industrial chemical in both warfare and homes. When allowed to mix with oxygen, it forms phosgene gas, which was one of the deadly gases used as a weapon in World War I (1914–1918). Today, it is used as an industrial solvent and as the cooling fluid in refrigerators. For many decades, it was part of various cosmetics and medicines, but the EPA banned its use in such products in 1976 when it became clear that chloroform could cause cancer.

A little bit of chloroform is produced by nature whenever chlorine is added to water that contains some organic matter. But most people accept that a slightly increased risk of cancer is a small price to pay for the greater safety from disease given by the chlorination of water.

Acid at Work

Hydrogen chloride, HCl, is a colorless, poisonous gas. When it is dissolved in water, it forms hydrochloric acid, which is an important industrial chemical. For industrial use, hydrochloric acid usually does not have to be pure. Impure HCl is a yellowish, thick liquid commonly called muriatic acid.

With food, the process called pickling preserves food

At a steel-pickling plant, new steel is dipped into hydrochloric acid to clean it.

by soaking it in vinegar to prevent spoilage. It also usually changes the flavor, as in making pickles out of cucumbers. In the metal industry, however, pickling is the process of dipping an iron product into a chemical to remove the rust-like coating that develops on it. About one-fourth of the many tons of hydrochloric acid produced in the United States is used for pickling steel. Once the rust has been removed, the steel can be plated to protect it.

A very different use of hydrogen chloride is in Novocain. This is the local anesthetic that dentists often use when they are drilling teeth down into the nerves. The drug leaves the mouth feeling numb and swollen for a few hours afterward, but it prevents pain during drilling, making going to the dentist a less frightening experience than it might otherwise be.

POISON IN THE WORLD OF THE BROTHERS GRIMM

Soldiers and their horses in World War I had to wear gas masks to protect themselves from chlorine-based chemical weapons.

A science writer, Rachel Carson, is often credited with alerting the public to the dangers to the environment presented by many chemicals. For many people, Carson's 1962 book, *Silent Spring,* was how they learned that the use of the poisons called insecticides, which were invented to kill insect pests, also killed birds. She wrote that the "world of systemic insecticides is a weird world, surpassing the imaginings of the brothers Grimm."

In the following years, the world became even "Grimmer," as new and very powerful chemicals, often containing chlorine, were invented for a specific purpose and then found to cause serious harm to the environment. Humanity will be dealing with those chemicals and making choices about their use for many years to come.

Killing with Chlorine

Chlorine, Cl_2, was first used as a chemical weapon in 1915, during World War I, in combat at Ypres, France. The gas mask was invented as a defense, but it was too late for many soldiers, who had already breathed in so much of the gas that their lungs were damaged for the rest of their lives.

Unlike chlorine gas, which has a recognizable pungent odor, the chemical called phosgene, $COCl_2$, does not give off a disturbing odor. It has been described as smelling like freshly cut hay. A victim can inhale enough phosgene to kill without even realizing it. Phosgene does not kill immediately. Instead, the victim dies several days later of pulmonary edema (swelling of the lung tissues). Today, phosgene is used in the manufacture of certain plastics.

Police and soldiers still use chlorine in weapons such as certain kinds of tear gas. The chemical in the tear gas known as Mace is officially known as 2-chloroacetophenone. Sprayed in the faces of muggers or rioting mobs, it stops people in their tracks, leaving them coughing, choking, and unable to see because the chemical causes quick, painful tearing of the eyes.

Mustard gas, which was also used in World War I, is a combination of chlorine and sulfur that smells like mustard. It blisters the skin and burns the eyes. Many soldiers who fell victim to it suffered problems all their lives. The worst problem with mustard gas in war is that it can penetrate clothing, even rubber boots, without the victim realizing that he has been attacked until his skin starts to burn. The chemical remains on the ground, where someone coming along the next day can fall victim to it.

Killing Pests

Although many serious diseases were almost eliminated by the use of chlorine in water, other diseases carried by insects continued to kill people in large numbers. Typhus, for example, is carried by lice. Malaria and yellow fever are carried by mosquitoes. Bubonic plague is carried by fleas. Before World War II, more soldiers died of these diseases than died in battle. But a chemical discovered just as the war was starting changed that. The Allies (the United States, Great Britain, and the Soviet Union) obtained a small sample of a white powder invented in Switzerland, which they gave the code name G4.

G4 is better known today as DDT. It is the common name for dichlorodiphenyltrichloroethane, which has the complex formula $CCl_3CH(C_6H_4Cl)_2$. As far as is known, the molecule was first produced by a chemistry student named Othmer Zeidler in 1874. Experimenting with several different chemicals, he produced a white crystal. He wrote up the results of his experiment, but no one paid any attention for more than 50 years.

In 1945, officials in New York proudly sprayed the beaches on Long Island with the new chemical DDT to eliminate insect pests. No one thought that the spray might be dangerous.

In 1939, chemist Paul Herman Müller, working at the Swiss firm of Geigy, repeated the experiment. Müller was looking for insecticides, and he discovered that the white crystal was a compound that, even in very low doses, would kill harmful insects.

After the war, the ease of making DDT and its amazing effectiveness made it a vital chemical all around the world. In 1948, Müller received a Nobel Prize in medicine for his discovery.

DDT apparently works on the nerve cells in the insects. In animals, electrolytes have specific locations where they act as they are intended to do. In the wrong locations, they are harmful. The DDT molecule takes advantage of this fact by opening the membrane around nerve cells and allowing sodium ions to flow in. Since sodium controls the firing of the nerve cells, the surplus sodium makes the nerve cells fire repeatedly until they die. Then the insect itself dies.

DDT was soon used throughout the world and praised for the ease with which it destroyed malaria-carrying mosquitoes. It had the great additional benefit of not reacting to other chemicals in the environment so that it lasted, or persisted, for long periods of time. This insecticide opened a whole new era in agricultural chemistry. For the first time, there was a way to fight the pests that could destroy whole crops.

Unforeseen Results

Bad news was around the corner, though. DDT was developed specifically to keep its effectiveness for a long time, to not change or break down easily. That is also its most serious drawback—DDT lingers in the environment. Once in the water and soil, it was there to stay.

As noted by Rachel Carson, DDT was reducing bird populations. DDT harmed birds' ability to produce strong eggshells. Their shells were becoming too thin to keep chicks alive long enough to hatch. Carson called DDT the "elixir of death."

The shell of this broken pelican egg was not strong enough to survive the growth of the baby bird inside because DDT in the food chain weakened the eggshell.

DDT is manufactured by heating chlorobenzene and chloral hydrate in the presence of sulfuric acid. The result is DDT and water. It is the most famous of the organochlorines, which are sometimes called chlorinated hydrocarbons. Other chlorinated hydrocarbons include carbon tetrachloride, trichloroethylene, and chloroform, as well as the insecticides lindane and aldrin. In developed countries, most chlorinated hydrocarbons have been replaced by pesticides that do less damage to the environment. In less developed countries, however, where disease, especially malaria, is still rampant, DDT is still the pesticide of choice.

DDT does not work as well as it once did. Within ten years after its first use as an insecticide, insects had already begun to develop immunity to it. These insects contain an enzyme that removes a chlorine atom from the DDT molecule, destroying its ability to poison. The use of DDT was banned in the United States in 1972, and most other countries have reduced its use.

A Bad Breed of Chemicals

Like DDT, chlorinated hydrocarbons have entered the environment and are now found in air, water, and living things. They get into our bodies from the fish we eat. Even far from industrial cities, in the Arctic, polar bears and walruses have been found to have organochlorines in their bodies.

So far, at least 170 different organochlorine chemicals have been identified in our bodies, especially in fat, where they accumulate. These chemicals, which play such a huge role in modern life, are thought to be carcinogenic. Among the chemicals that get the most attention from the public are such "alphabet-soup" chemicals as PCBs, TCDDs, and CFCs.

PCBs

Polychlorinated biphenyls, known as PCBs, are chemicals that were developed in the 1920s and 1930s to be used in electrical equipment. Each kind of PCB contains a different number of chlorine atoms in the complex molecule. All of them, though, are nonflammable and good electrical insulators. Their use almost eliminated electrical fires in schools and office buildings.

But once again, a good thing turned out to have a downside. The chemical plants where PCBs were made and the manufacturing plants where they were used, as well as the waste dumps where the products they were used in were thrown away—all of these were found in the 1960s to be killing living things.

PCBs entered the food chain, often by being dumped in water. They gradually accumulated in the bodies of animals higher up the food chain. It was suspected that, as was the case with birds' eggs and DDT, PCBs affected the reproductive ability of the animals ingesting them. The birth rate went down, and many baby animals were born with birth defects that kept them from growing and reproducing normally.

The United States stopped making PCBs in 1977, but it was too late. They were already virtually everywhere in the environment. Among the largest hazardous-waste sites scheduled for cleanup in the United States are rivers and bays where PCBs were dumped many decades ago. These chemicals have become part of the sediment at the bottom of such bodies of water. So long as they remain there, life in the river is endangered.

Fortunately, once they are retrieved from river bottoms (an expensive process), PCBs can be burned to dispose of these chemicals. Heat breaks the molecules down into carbon dioxide, water, and hydrogen chloride. The hydrogen chloride can be "scrubbed," or diluted, and disposed of harmlessly.

Dioxins

Unlike DDT and PCBs, the group of chlorinated hydrocarbons called dioxins (and related ones called furans) have no beneficial use. They are not manufactured for a specific purpose. Instead, they occur as an unwanted by-product in the production of other chemicals or from burning. There are at least 210 varieties of dioxins, and about 10 percent of them are regarded as very poisonous.

A dioxin was found in Agent Orange, a mixture of powerful chemicals used by American troops in Vietnam to make jungle trees lose their leaves so that the enemy could not hide there. Soldiers and citizens exposed to Agent Orange experienced miscarriages, birth defects, and cancers far above the usual number.

A dioxin was also a by-product in making a useful antiseptic cleanser and deodorizer called hexachlorophene. It was available commercially, and many people liked it for its ability to fight acne, but it was eventually taken off the market.

These technicians are using a special pump to remove PCBs from an electrical transformer and refill it with an oil that does not contain PCBs.

Scientists now know that dioxins form naturally wherever burning takes place, even in home fireplaces. There are dioxins in cigarette smoke. The actual level of dioxin in cigarette smoke is quite low. However, smokers (and nearby nonsmokers) end up inhaling the same dioxins over and over because they usually breathe the same smoke-filled air that they have just exhaled. Cigarette smoke actually contains probably 4,000 different compounds, and at least 50 of them are carcinogenic.

The public is most concerned about one specific dioxin known as TCDD. In 1971, oil containing the chemical was sprayed on the roads around Times Beach, Missouri, to keep down dust. Biologists found that this dioxin produced terrible birth defects in certain laboratory animals and feared that it might do the same to humans. The federal government paid residents to move away, and the town was evacuated.

Nine years later, though, the government official who called for the evacuation admitted that he had been wrong. He had realized that dioxins were not nearly so serious a threat as he had thought. The massive doses used on laboratory guinea pigs did not translate into similar damage to humans. It did not even translate into similar damage to hamsters, which are related to guinea pigs. Oddly, guinea pigs are 3,000 to 5,000 times more sensitive to dioxins than hamsters are.

The Italian Experience

This does not mean that TCDD is safe. In 1976, a factory exploded in Seveso, Italy, sending TCDD raining into the environment. Twenty-five years later, studies made of the population showed that those men who had received the greatest exposure to the dioxin fathered many fewer sons than those who had not been exposed. Apparently the hazardous poison interrupted the transmission of endocrine hormones in men, especially in men exposed to the chemical before they were 20 years old.

The differences did not just concern the ratio of boys to girls. Of the children who were born, there was an increase of 40 percent in the rate of birth defects. Of adults exposed to the chemical, there was a significant increase in the number of cases of certain kinds of cancer, especially in women.

No one really knows yet just how humans react to TCDD and at what level of exposure. The National Toxicology Program of the Department of Health and Human Services prepares lists of known carcinogens, and they have been on the verge of including TCDD for several years. As the 21st century started, there was still strong disagreement about the danger from TCDD and other dioxins.

Scientists have found a protein in human cells to which dioxins can bind and begin the damage that might eventually change cells. They do not know yet what the normal function of this protein is or how great an exposure to dioxins is necessary for the change to occur. This uncertainty is the reason many people oppose the construction of incinerators to burn municipal trash.

CFCs in the Atmosphere

Chemicals called chlorofluorocarbons, or CFCs, were invented for use in refrigeration systems in the 1930s. They were called "wonder chemicals" because they were inexpensive, did not flame, did not explode or burn in shipping, and cooled by evaporation. The most common CFC, known by the trade name Freon, was used in home and automobile air-conditioning systems for years. As these systems were repaired, the old Freon was released into the atmosphere, and new Freon was put in.

CFCs were also used as the propellant gas in spray cans. When the button on a can was pressed, the CFC came out, carrying with it the chemical that was being used, such as hair spray, deodorant, paint, or whatever. The propellant gas went into the atmosphere. CFCs have also been used as the gas that makes the plastic called polyurethane foam into the hardened material used in packaging and coffee cups. Each time some of that material is broken, the gas is released into the atmosphere.

Because CFCs did not react with other chemicals, they seemed to be stable and not particularly hazardous. However,

These are models of the different CFC molecules. Chlorine atoms, some of which are hidden in these models, are shown in dark green.

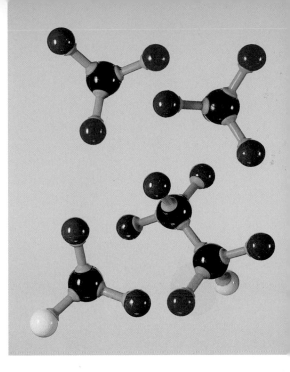

chemists had not taken into account the fact that although CFCs do not react with other chemicals, they do react to light. For several decades, no one knew that when these wonder chemicals rose through the atmosphere into the stratosphere, they were being broken apart by sunlight.

Destruction of the Ozone Layer

CFCs harmed the atmosphere in two ways. First, they damaged the ozone layer in the stratosphere. The ozone layer is a region of O_3 (triatomic oxygen) molecules that lies between 10 and 50 kilometers (6 and 30 miles) above Earth. Ozone has the useful ability to absorb ultraviolet (UV) radiation, thus keeping most of it from striking us on Earth. UV radiation is harmful to living things. UV radiation causes sunburns, for example, which can lead to skin cancer.

Stable CFC molecules drift upward through the atmosphere to the ozone layer. There, they are struck by ultraviolet radiation and finally begin to break down, releasing a chlorine atom. The freed chlorine atom reacts with ozone, O_3, to produce chlorine oxide and regular diatomic oxygen. Chlorine oxide molecules react with loose oxygen atoms to turn into plain chlorine again, ready to do more damage. The original ozone molecule, which helped to protect Earth, is gone and cannot be regenerated.

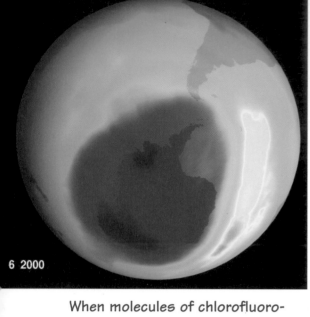

6 2000

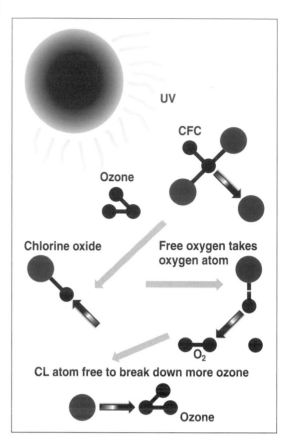

When molecules of chlorofluoro-carbons (CFCs) rise to the stratosphere, a chemical reaction occurs that is gradually destroying the protective ozone layer. The "hole" in the ozone layer over the Antarctic is clearly seen in the satellite photo above.

O_2, the normal diatomic oxygen molecule, has no ability to absorb ultraviolet radiation. Instead, these harmful rays now strike Earth. They are especially strong beneath the so-called "holes" in the ozone that form each winter over the polar regions. The skin-cancer rate in Australia, for example, has risen dramatically in recent decades.

The second way in which CFCs are harmful is that they contribute to global warming. The molecules in the atmosphere that absorb heat—and consequently raise the temperature of the whole planet—are those that consist of several atoms, such as carbon dioxide, CO_2; methane, CH_4; and nitrous oxide, N_2O.

DuPont, one of the largest manufacturers of CFCs in the world, stopped all production of CFCs by 1999. In industry, they have largely been replaced by hydrofluorocarbons, or HFCs, which clearly do not contain chlorine. Unfortunately, the CFCs already in the stratosphere will continue to do their damage for many years to come.

Is ClO_2 the Answer?

Clearly, chlorine itself in the environment is not the major problem. It's the chemicals that chlorine forms, either with the help of humans or accidentally.

Chemists long thought that organochlorine and related compounds were produced only by human activities. Now they know that many living things produce them as well. Some sea creatures, such as sponges and corals, for example, produce organochlorines naturally, as do some bacteria and algae (primitive one-celled plants). Thus we cannot avoid them.

While humans can do little about natural organochlorines, something can be done about human-produced organochlorines. One answer appears to be using chlorine dioxide instead of pure chlorine. Chlorine dioxide has the benefits of chlorine without its bad aspects. And, most importantly, chlorine dioxide does not form organochlorines.

Another advantage of chlorine dioxide over chlorine is that less is needed to treat water and so it has a lower environmental impact. It does an even better job because it has 2.6 times the oxidizing capacity of chlorine. Unlike Cl_2, ClO_2 kills germs in water or other materials that are both acid and basic. Chlorine dioxide cannot be shipped under pressure, so it must be produced at the place where it is used. As a result, there is less likelihood of accidents.

One thing is certain about using chemicals containing chlorine: more must be learned about new ones before they are used in large amounts. History tells us that what we don't know about chemicals can seriously hurt us.

A CHLORINE CATALOG

Saving Mothers

Perhaps the first use of chlorine to kill dangerous bacteria was carried out by a physician in Vienna, Austria, in the mid-1840s. More than other doctors at his hospital, Dr. Ignaz Semmelweis was troubled by the number of women who died giving birth. When women had their babies at home, very few of them died. It had to have something to do with the hospital itself, or with the people in it.

Semmelweis observed that the death rate was a lot higher in the section of the hospital where the women were examined and treated by medical students than it was in the ward where they were cared for by women called midwives. The only real difference he could find was that the medical students did their examinations right after working with dead bodies. Perhaps they

Doctors today scrub their hands thoroughly with strong disinfectant soap before treating patients.

brought something into the hospital from the bodies.

Scorning the advice of the other doctors, Semmelweis insisted that the medical students wash their hands in chlorine before they touched women patients. The death rate fell dramatically. Even so, other doctors ridiculed him, and he lost his position at the hospital over his insistence that all people should wash their hands in the chlorinated water. It was several decades before doctors everywhere agreed with Semmelweis that germs could cause disease and death.

A Newer Way to Save Lives

One of the earliest antibiotics, or bacteria-killing medicines, was chloramphenicol, which, as its name indicates, contains chlorine. It is especially useful against typhoid fever. However, it turned out to have a bad side effect of damaging the marrow of bones, where blood cells are formed. This antibiotic is better known as Chloromycetin.

Chloramphenicol and the similar chlortetracycline were developed in the early 1940s, when antibiotics were still new. They are called broad-spectrum antibiotics, meaning that they are useful against a broad range of bacteria. For most purposes, they have been replaced by newer ones, but they still have their uses. Chlortetracycline, better known as Aureomycin, for example, is useful against brucellosis, an infectious fever that is caught by both humans and domestic animals.

The Peru Tragedy

In the late 1980s, officials in Lima, Peru, shut down some of the chlorinators in the water supply in Lima and neighboring communities. They had decided that the formation of chloroform and other hazardous compounds during the chlorination of water was serious enough to justify their act.

Within months, an outbreak of cholera began in the northern

suburbs of Lima. It rapidly became an epidemic, the first cholera outbreak in South America in more than a century. Within 23 months, a total of 731,312 cases of cholera had been recorded. They resulted in 6,323 deaths. One-third of the deaths occurred within Lima itself.

No matter how serious the production of some harmful chemicals in chlorinated water might be, the risk cannot be nearly as serious as the death toll from cutting off the chlorinators. The Peruvian officials had made a very bad decision.

Mickey Finn

Chloral hydrate, $CCl_3CH(OH)_2$, is used in manufacturing DDT. But 100 years ago, it was well known as a sleeping medicine, or sedative. A few drops in a drink knocked a person out so quickly that it became a favorite plot device of mystery writers. A dose of chloral hydrate given in a drink has been popularly called a Mickey Finn. It may have received this name from a bar in Chicago, where, in the early days of the twentieth century, drinkers were sometimes knocked out and robbed.

With Help from a Chlorine Atom

Chlorpromazine (also known as Thorazine) is a tranquilizer that has been used since the 1950s to calm mentally ill patients, especially those who suffer from the serious mental disorder known as schizophrenia. Interestingly, a similar drug called promazine does not contain the chlorine atom in its structure and it is not nearly as effective in making life livable for those stricken with mental disorders.

Getting Off Drugs

Heroin is an illegal drug to which a person can become addicted, often requiring him or her to do whatever is necessary to get more. One of the methods doctors use to break a heroin addiction is to replace the heroin with a chemical called methadone, or dolophine hydrochloride. Methadone was originally used to relieve pain. Like heroin, it is addictive, but it does not result in the psychological high that makes heroin so difficult to stop using.

Ringing Ears and Fireworks

In the late 18th century, potassium chlorate, $KClO_3$, was manufactured for use as an explosive. It is still used today in making fireworks. A teacher once wrote of his first experience of experimenting with potassium chlorate, which can be a mild disinfectant when rubbed on skin. He combined the $KClO_3$ with the element phosphorus (P, element #15).

"For three days my ears were ringing," the teacher recorded in his journal. "The open dish was shattered, the shards had penetrated the desk, and despite a zealous

Potassium chlorate is one of the basic explosive ingredients in many different kinds of fireworks.

search absolutely nothing was to be found of the horn spoon except the handle, which was in my hand."

That's a terribly dramatic—and very dangerous—way to learn about the explosive qualities of potassium chlorate. Chlorine compounds such as potassium chlorate or potassium perchlorate are used in fireworks because the chlorine in them reacts with various metals to produce light of different colors. Strontium chloride, for example, emits a red light, while barium chloride produces green light, and copper chloride produces blue light.

Metal Underarms

Aluminum chloride, $AlCl_3$, is one of the main ingredients in antiperspirants. The aluminum ions are released in the wetness under the arms and act to close sweat ducts in the skin. They also kill bacteria in the sweat, eliminating underarm odor. Used differently, aluminum chloride reacts with sodium to yield aluminum metal. The chloride ions transfer from the aluminum to the sodium, leaving metallic aluminum.

Needing to Breathe

Chlorate candles are chemical devices that can be stored for a long time and still provide oxygen in an emergency. Such a candle is usually part of a breathing apparatus that an emergency worker, such as a firefighter, dons to work in smoke. These candles contain chlorates and perchlorates, which when ignited, give off oxygen for emergency breathing.

$$2NaClO_3 + flame \rightarrow 2NaCl \text{ (salt)} + 3O_2$$

Surprise!

It may seem extraordinary, even alarming, to chocolate lovers, but an 11.3-gram (4-ounce) chocolate bar contains 270 milligrams of chlorine.

Clams and Chlorine

One of the odder (and more devastating) environmental problems of the late twentieth century was the accidental introduction of a species of Asiatic clam and zebra mussel from other countries into the waters of the United States. These new species seem to have no natural enemies in American waters. They have overwhelmed native clams and mussels and are spreading throughout the interior waters of North America, where they are also damaging the water-intake pipes of municipal water-supply systems.

A solution has been found in the normal processes of making water drinkable by the public—chlorination. Although the chlorine used to purify water does not affect the adult clams and mussels, it does prevent the larval stages of these animals from growing. The advantage of stopping these invaders from elsewhere will have to be weighed against the use of extra chlorine in water sources.

Zebra mussels clogged this water-intake pipe. Chlorine may play a role in preventing these pests from taking over more rivers and lakes.

Chlorine in Brief

Name: chlorine, from the Greek word *chloros*, meaning "greenish-yellow"

Symbol: Cl

Discoverer: First isolated by Carl Wilhelm Scheele in 1774 but not identified as an element until 1810 by Humphry Davy

Atomic number: 17

Atomic weight: 35.453

Electrons in the shells: 2, 8, 7

Group: 17, also called VIIA, the halogens; other elements in Group 17 with 7 electrons in the outer shell include fluorine, bromine, iodine, and astatine

Usual characteristics: a greenish-yellow poisonous gas that exists as a diatomic (two-atom) molecule that reacts readily with other elements

Density (mass per unit volume): 3.21 grams per cubic centimeter as a gas, 1.56 as a liquid

Melting point (freezing point): −101.5 °C (−150.7 °F)

Boiling point (liquefaction point): −34.04 °C (−29.27 °F)

Abundance:

Earth − 20th most abundant element

Earth's crust − at 0.19% the 11th most abundant element

Human body − 0.15% by weight (same as sodium), smallest of the macronutrients

Seawater − 18,000 ppm, or 2 percent by weight

Stable isotopes: 75.77% of natural chlorine is Cl-35; the remainder is Cl-37

Radioactive isotopes: Cl-36 and the series Cl-38 to Cl-43

Glossary

acid: definitions vary, but basically it is a corrosive substance that gives up a positive hydrogen ion (H+), equal to a proton when dissolved in water; indicates less than 7 on the pH scale because of its large number of hydrogen ions

alkali: a substance, such as an hydroxide or carbonate of an alkali metal, that when dissolved in water causes an increase in the hydroxide ion (OH-) concentration, forming a basic solution

anion: an ion with a negative charge

atom: the smallest amount of an element that exhibits the properties of the element, consisting of protons, electrons, and (usually) neutrons

base: a substance that accepts a hydrogen ion (H+) when dissolved in water; indicates higher than 7 on the pH scale because of its small number of hydrogen ions

boiling point: the temperature at which a liquid at normal pressure evaporates into a gas, or a solid changes directly (sublimes) into a gas

bond: the attractive force linking atoms together in a molecule or crystal

catalyst: a substance that causes or speeds a chemical reaction without itself being consumed in the reaction

cation: an ion with a positive charge

chemical reaction: a transformation or change in a substance involving the electrons of the chemical elements making up the substance

compound: a substance formed by two or more chemical elements bound together by chemical means

covalent bond: a link between two atoms made by the atoms sharing electrons

crystal: a solid substance in which the atoms are arranged in three-dimensional patterns that create smooth outer surfaces, or faces

decompose: to break down a substance into its components

density: the amount of material in a given volume, or space; mass per unit volume; often stated as grams per cubic centimeter (g/cm^3)

diatomic: made up of two atoms

dissolve: to spread evenly throughout the volume of another substance

distillation: the process in which a liquid is heated until it evaporates and the gas is collected and condensed back into a liquid in another container; often used to separate mixtures into their different components

electrode: a device such as a metal plate that conducts electrons into or out of a solution or battery

electrolysis: the decomposition of a substance by electricity

electrolyte: a substance that when dissolved in water or when liquefied conducts electricity

element: a substance that cannot be split chemically into simpler substances that maintain the same characteristics. Each of the 103 naturally occurring chemical elements is made up of atoms of the same kind.

evaporate: to change from a liquid to a gas

gas: a state of matter in which the atoms or molecules move freely, matching the shape and volume of the container holding it

group: a vertical column in the Periodic Table, with each element having similar physical and chemical characteristics; also called chemical family

half-life: the period of time required for half of a radioactive element to decay

hormone: any of various secretions of the endocrine glands that control different functions of the body, especially at the cellular level

ion: an atom or molecule that has acquired an electric charge by gaining or losing one or more electrons

ionic bond: a link between two atoms made by one atom taking one or more electrons from the other, giving the two atoms opposite electrical charges, which holds them together

isotope: an atom with a different number of neutrons in its nucleus from other atoms of the same element

mass number: the total of protons and neutrons in the nucleus of an atom

melting point: the temperature at which a solid becomes a liquid

metal: a chemical element that conducts electricity, usually shines, or reflects light, is dense, and can be shaped. About three-quarters of the naturally occurring elements are metals.

metalloid: a chemical element that has some characteristics of a metal and some of a nonmetal; includes some elements in Groups 13 through 17 in the Periodic Table

molecule: the smallest amount of a substance that has the characteristics of the substance and usually consists of two or more atoms

monomer: a molecule that can be linked to many other identical molecules to make a polymer

neutral: 1) having neither acidic nor basic properties; 2) having no electrical charge

neutron: a subatomic particle within the nucleus of all atoms except hydrogen; has no electric charge

nonmetal: a chemical element that does not conduct electricity, is not dense, and is too brittle to be worked. Nonmetals easily form ions, and they include some elements in Groups 14 through 17 and all of Group 18 in the Periodic Table.

nucleus: 1) the central part of an atom, which has a positive electrical charge from its one or more protons; the nuclei of all atoms except hydrogen also include electrically neutral neutrons; 2) the central portion of most living cells, which controls the activities of the cells and contains the genetic material

organic: containing carbon

oxidation: the loss of electrons during a chemical reaction; need not necessarily involve the element oxygen

pH: a measure of the acidity of a substance, on a scale of 0 to 14, with 7 being neutral. pH stands for "potential of hydrogen."

pressure: the force exerted by an object divided by the area over which the force is exerted. The air at sea level exerts a pressure, called atmospheric pressure, of 14.7 pounds per square inch (1013 millibars).

proton: a subatomic particle within the nucleus of all atoms; has a positive electric charge

radical: an atom or molecule that contains an unpaired electron

radioactive: of an atom, spontaneously emitting high-energy particles

reduction: the gain of electrons, which occurs in conjunction with oxidation

respiration: the process of taking in oxygen and giving off carbon dioxide

salt: any compound that, with water, results from the neutralization of an acid by a base. In common usage, sodium chloride (table salt)

shell: a region surrounding the nucleus of an atom in which one or more electrons can occur. The inner shell can hold a maximum of two electrons; others may hold eight or more. If an atom's outer, or valence, shell does not hold its maximum number of electrons, the atom is subject to chemical reactions.

solid: a state of matter in which the shape of the collection of atoms or molecules does not depend on the container

solution: a mixture in which one substance is evenly distributed throughout another

sublime: to change directly from a solid to a gas without becoming a liquid first

synthetic: created in a laboratory instead of occurring naturally

ultraviolet: electromagnetic radiation which has a wavelength shorter than visible light

valence electron: an electron located in the outer shell of an atom, available to participate in chemical reactions

vitamin: any of several organic substances, usually obtainable from a balanced diet, that the human body needs for specific physiological processes to take place

For Further Information

BOOKS

Atkins, P. W. *The Periodic Kingdom: A Journey into the Land of the Chemical Elements.* NY: Basic Books, 1995

Emsley, John. *Molecules at an Exhibition: Portraits of Intriguing Materials in Everyday Life.* Oxford: Oxford University Press, 1998

Heiserman, David L. *Exploring Chemical Elements and Their Compounds,* Blue Ridge Summit, PA: Tab Books, 1992

Hoffman, Roald, and Vivian Torrence. *Chemistry Imagined: Reflections on Science.* Washington, DC: Smithsonian Institution Press, 1993

Newton, David E. *Chemical Elements: From Carbon to Krypton.* 3 volumes. Detroit: UXL, 1998

CD-ROM

Discover the Elements: The Interactive Periodic Table of the Chemical Elements, Paradigm Interactive, Greensboro, NC, 1995

INTERNET SITES

Note that useful sites on the Internet can change and even disappear. If the following site addresses do not work, use a search engine that you find useful, such as:
Yahoo:

http://www.yahoo.com

or Google:

http://google.com

or Encyclopaedia Britannica:

http://britannica.com

A very thorough listing of the major characteristics, uses, and compounds of all the chemical elements can be found at a site called WebElements:

http://www.web-elements.com

Many subjects are covered on WWW Virtual Library. It also includes a useful collection of links to other sites:

http://www.earthsystems.org/Environment/shtml

INDEX